Fortinet NSE4 6. 2 Actual Exam Actual Questions 2021

Judd Robertson

Fortinet NSE4_FGT-6.2 Exam Actual Questions

Question #1

Examine the FortiGate configuration:

```
config user settings
    set auth-on-demand implicitly
end
```

What will happen to unauthenticated users when an active authentication policy is followed by a fall through policy without authentication?

1. The user must log in again to authenticate.
2. The user will be denied access to resources without authentication.
3. The user will not be prompted for authentication.
4. User authentication happens at an interface level.

Correct Answer(s): 3

Question #2

Which downstream FortiGate VDOM is used to join the Security Fabric when split-task VDOM is enabled on all FortiGate devices?

1. FG-traffic VDOM
2. Root VDOM
3. Customer VDOM
4. Global VDOM

Question #3

In an HA cluster operating in active-active mode, which path is taken by the SYN packet of an HTTP session that is offloaded to a secondary FortiGate?

1. Client > secondary FortiGate > primary FortiGate > web server
2. Client > primary FortiGate > secondary FortiGate > primary FortiGate > web server
3. Client > primary FortiGate > secondary FortiGate > web server
4. Client > secondary FortiGate > web server

Question #4

Which two statements about antivirus scanning mode are true? (Choose two.)

1. In proxy-based inspection mode, antivirus buffers the whole file for scanning, before sending it to the client.
2. In full scan flow-based inspection mode, FortiGate buffers the file, but also simultaneously transmits it to the client.
3. In proxy-based inspection mode, files bigger than the buffer size are scanned.
4. In quick scan mode, you can configure antivirus profiles to use any of the available antivirus signature databases.

Correct Answer(s): 1, 2

Question #5

The FSSO collector agent set to advanced access mode for the Windows Active Directory uses which convention?

1. LDAP
2. Windows
3. RSSO
4. NTLM

Correct Answer(s): 1

Question #6

Which two statements about virtual domains (VDOMs) are true? (Choose two.)

1. Transparent mode and NAT mode VDOMs cannot be combined on the same FortiGate.
2. Each VDOM can be configured with different system hostnames.
3. Different VLAN subinterfaces of the same physical interface can be assigned to different VDOMs.
4. Each VDOM has its own routing table.

Correct Answer(s): 3, 4

Question #7

What three FortiGate components are tested during the hardware test? (Choose three.)

1. CPU
2. Administrative access
3. HA heartbeat
4. Hard disk
5. Network interfaces

Correct Answer(s): 1, 4, 5

Question #8

A team manager has decided that, while some members of the team need access to a particular website, the majority of the team does not.

Which configuration option is the most effective way to support this request?

1. Implement web filter authentication for the specified website.
2. Implement a web filter category override for the specified website.
3. Implement DNS filter for the specified website.
4. Implement web filter quotas for the specified website.

Correct Answer(s): 2

Question #9

Examine the exhibit, which shows the output of a web filtering real time debug.

```
Local-FortiGate # diagnose  debug enable

Local-FortiGate # diagnose debug application urlfilter -1

Local-FortiGate # msg="received a request /tmp/.wad_192_0_0.url.socket, addr_len
=31: d=www.bing.com:80, id=29, vfname='root', vfid=0, profile='default', type=0,
 client=10.0.1.10, url_source=1, url="/"
Url matches local rating
action=10(ftgd-block) wf-act=3(BLOCK) user="N/A" src=10.0.1.10 sport=63683 dst=2
04.79.197.200 dport=80 service="http" cat=26 cat_desc="Malicious Websites" hostn
ame="www.bing.com" url="/"
```

Why is the site www.bing.com being blocked?

1. The web site www.bing.com is categorized by FortiGuard as Malicious Websites.
2. The user has not authenticated with the FortiGate yet.
3. The web server IP address 204.79.197.200 is categorized by FortiGuard as Malicious Websites.
4. The rating for the web site www.bing.com has been locally overridden to a category that is being blocked.

Correct Answer(s): 4

Question #10

When using WPAD DNS method, which FQDN format do browsers use to query the DNS server?

1. srv_proxy.<local-domain>/wpad.dat
2. srv_tcp.wpad.<local-domain>
3. wpad.<local-domain>
4. proxy.<local-domain>.wpad

Correct Answer(s): 3

Question #11

Consider a new IPsec deployment with the following criteria:

☞ All satellite offices must connect to the two HQ sites.

☞ The satellite offices do not need to communicate directly with other satellite offices.

☞ Backup VPN is not required.

☞ The design should minimize the number of tunnels being configured.

Which topology should you use to satisfy all of the requirements?

1. Partial mesh
2. Redundant
3. Full mesh
4. Hub-and-spoke

Correct Answer(s): 4

Question #12

What criteria does FortiGate use to look for a matching firewall policy to process traffic? (Choose two.)

1. Services defined in the firewall policy.
2. Incoming and outgoing interfaces
3. Highest to lowest priority defined in the firewall policy.
4. Lowest to highest policy ID number.

Correct Answer(s): 1, 2

Question #13

Refer to the exhibit.

You are configuring the root FortiGate to implement the Security Fabric. You are configuring port10 to communicate with a downstream FortiGate. The exhibit shows the default Edit Interface.

When configuring the root FortiGate to communicate with a downstream FortiGate, which two settings must you configure? (Choose two.)

1. Enable Device Detection
2. Administrative Access: FortiTelemetry.
3. IP/Network Mask.
4. Role: Security Fabric.

Correct Answer(s): 2, 3

Question #14

Which two statements about NTLM authentication are correct? (Choose two.)

1. It requires DC agents on every domain controller when used in multidomain environments.
2. It is useful when users log in to DCs that are not monitored by a collector agent.
3. It requires NTLM-enabled web browsers.
4. It takes over as the primary authentication method when configured alongside FSSO.

Correct Answer(s): 2, 3

Question #15

Refer to the exhibit.

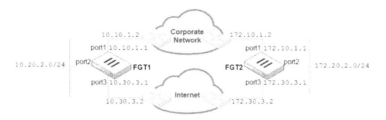

A firewall administrator must configure equal cost multipath (ECMP) routing on FGT1 to ensure both port1 and port3 links are used, at the same time, for all traffic destined for 172.20.2.0/24.

8

Given the network diagram shown in the exhibit, which two static routes will satisfy this requirement on FGT1? (Choose two.)

1. 172.20.2.0/24 [1/0] via 10.10.1.2, port1 [0/0]
2. 172.20.2.0/24 [25/0] via 10.30.3.2, port3 [5/0]
3. 172.20.2.0/24 [25/0] via 10.10.1.2, port1 [5/0]
4. 172.20.2.0/24 [1/150] via 10.30.3.2, port3 [10/0]

Correct Answer(s): 2, 3

Question #16

On a FortiGate with a hard disk, how frequently can you upload logs to FortiAnalyzer or FortiManager? (Choose two.)

1. On-demand
2. Hourly
3. Every 5 minutes
4. In real time

Correct Answer(s): 3, 4

Question #17

Refer to the exhibit.

```
ike 0: comes 172.20.187.114:500->172.20.186.222:500,ifindex=2....
ike 0: IKEv1 exchange=Identity Protection id=4497f0b077c742b5/0000000000000000 len=296
ike 0:4497f0b077c742b5/0000000000000000:8: responder: main mode get 1st message...
...
ike 0:4497f0b077c742b5/0000000000000000:8: SA proposal chosen, matched gateway Remote
ike 0: found Remote 172.20.186.222 2 -> 172.20.187.114:500
...
ike 0:Remote:8: sent IKE msg (ident_r1send): 172.20.186.222:500->172.20.187.114:500, len=160
ike 0: comes 172.20.187.114:500->172.20.186.222:500,ifindex=2....
ike 0:Remote:8: responder:main mode get 2nd message...
....
ike 0:Remote:8: sent IKE msg (ident_r2send): 172.20.186.222:500->172.20.187.114:500, len=292
ike 0:Remote:8: ISAKMP SA 4497f0b077c742b5/fbbb59b259a0fc3e key 24:DCD18FBE7CFA138E27B06F
ike 0: comes 172.20.187.114:500->172.20.186.222:500,ifindex=2....
ike 0:Remote:8: responder: main mode get 3rd message...
...
ike 0:Remote:8: PSK authentication succeeded
ike 0:Remote:8: authentication OK
ike 0:Remote:8: established IKE SA 4497f0b077c742b5/fbbb59b259a0fc3e
```

Given the partial output of an IKE real-time debug shown in the exhibit, which statement about the output is true?

1. The VPN is configured to use pre-shared key authentication.
2. Extended authentication (XAuth) was successful.
3. Remote is the host name of the remote IPsec peer.
4. Phase 1 went down.

Correct Answer(s): 1

Question #18

An administrator needs to create an SSL-VPN connection for accessing an internal server using the bookmark, Port Forward.

Which step must the administrator take to successfully achieve this configuration?

1. Configure an SSL VPN realm for clients to use the Port Forward bookmark.
2. Configure the client application to forward IP traffic through FortiClient.
3. Configure the virtual IP address to be assigned to the SSL VPN users.

4. Configure the client application to forward IP traffic to a Java applet proxy.

Correct Answer(s): 4

Question #19

Which two static routes are not maintained in the routing table? (Choose two.)

1. Dynamic routes
2. Policy routes
3. Named Address routes
4. ISDB routes

Correct Answer(s): 2, 4

Question #20

An administrator wants to configure a FortiGate as a DNS server. FortiGate must use a DNS database first, and then relay all irresolvable queries to an external

DNS server. Which DNS method must you use?

1. Recursive
2. Non-recursive
3. Forward to primary and secondary DNS
4. Forward to system DNS

Correct Answer(s): 1

Question #21

Which two FortiGate configuration tasks will create a route in the policy route table? (Choose two.)

1. Creating an SD-WAN route for individual member interfaces
2. Creating an SD-WAN rule to route traffic based on link latency
3. Creating a static route with a named address object
4. Creating a static route with an Internet services object

Correct Answer(s): 2, 4

Question #22

Refer to the exhibits.

AV profile

Edit AntiVirus Profile

Name

Comments: Scan files and block viruses.

Scan Mode: Quick **Full**

Detect Viruses: **Block** Monitor

Inspected Protocols

HTTP
SMTP
POP3
IMAP
MAPI
FTP
CIFS

APT Protection Options

Content Disarm and Reconstruction
Treat Windows Executables in Email Attachments as Viruses
Include Mobile Malware Protection

Virus Outbreak Prevention
Use FortiGuard Outbreak Prevention Database
Use External Malware Block List

Name: default
Comments: All default services
Log Oversized Files
RPC over HTTP

Protocol Port Mapping

HTTP — Any Specify — 80
SMTP — Any Specify — 25
POP3 — Any Specify — 110
IMAP — Any Specify — 143
FTP — Any Specify — 21
NNTP — Any Specify — 119
MAPI — 135
DNS — 53

Common Options

Comfort Clients
Block Oversized File/Email

Web Options

Chunked Bypass
Add Fortinet Bar
HTTP Policy Redirect

Email Options

Allow Fragmented Messages
Append Signature (SMTP)

File transfer output

Given the antivirus profile and file transfer output shown in the exhibits, why is FortiGate not blocking the eicar.com file over FTP download?

13

1. Because the proxy options profile needs to scan FTP traffic on a non-standard port
2. Because the FortiSandbox signature database is required to successfully scan FTP traffic
3. Because deep-inspection must be enabled for FortiGate to fully scan FTP traffic
4. Because FortiGate needs to be operating in flow-based inspection mode in order to scan FTP traffic

Correct Answer(s): 1

Question #23

Refer to the exhibit.

Policy Lookup			
Source Interface	≈ port3	▼	
Protocol	TCP	▼	
Source	10.0.1.10		
Source Port	Optional (1-65535)	↕	
Destination	facebook.com		
Destination Port	443	↕	
		Search	Cancel

The exhibits show the firewall policies and the objects used in the firewall policies. The administrator is using the Policy Lookup feature and has entered the search criteria shown in the exhibit.

Based on the input criteria, which of the following will be highlighted?

1. The policy with ID 1
2. The policy with ID 5
3. The policies with ID 2 and 3
4. The policy with ID 4

Correct Answer(s): 2

Question #24

Refer to the exhibit.

```
id=2 line=4677 msg= "vd-root received a packet (proto=6, 66.171.121.44:80 ->10.200.1.1:49886) from port1
flag [S.], seq 3567496940, ack 2176715502, win 5840"
id=2 line=4739 msg= "Find an existing session, id-00007fc0, reply direction"
id=2 line=2733 msg= "DNAT 10.200.1.1:49886 -> 10.0.1.10:49886"
id=2 line=2582 msg= "find a route: flag=00000000 gw-10.0.1.10 via port3"
```

The exhibit shows the output from a debug flow.

Which two statements about the output are correct? (Choose two.)

1. The packet was allowed by the firewall policy with the ID 00007fc0.

15

2.   The source IP address of the packet was translated to 10.0.1.10.
3.   FortiGate received a TCP SYN/ACK packet.
4.   FortiGate routed the packet through port3.

Correct Answer(s): 3, 4

Question #25

What is required to create an inter-VDOM link between two VDOMs?

1.   At least one of the VDOMs must operate in NAT mode.
2.   Both VDOMs must operate in NAT mode.
3.   The inspection mode of at least one VDOM must be NGFW policy-based.
4.   The inspection mode of both VDOMs must match.

Correct Answer(s): 1

Question #26

What FortiGate configuration is required to actively prompt users for credentials?

1.   You must enable one or more protocols that support active authentication on a firewall policy.
2.   You must position the firewall policy for active authentication before a firewall policy for passive authentication
3.   You must assign users to a group for active authentication
4.   You must enable the Authentication setting on the firewall policy

Question #27

Refer to the exhibit.

⊤ Status	⊤ Name	⊤ Type	⊤ Virtual Domain	⊤ IP/Netmask
Physical (10)				
⊠	port1	⬇ Physical Interface	▲ VDOM2	10.200.1.1 255.255.0
⊠	port2	⬇ Physical Interface	⊕ VDOM1	
VDOM Link (3)				
⊟	InterVDOM	⊓⊐ VDOM Link	⊕ VDOM1, ▲ VDOM2	
	InterVDOM0	⊓⊐ VDOM Link Interface	⊕ VDOM1	
	InterVDOM1	⊓⊐ VDOM Link Interface	▲ VDOM2	10.0.1.254 255.255.255.0

The exhibit shows network configurations. VDOM1 is operating in transparent mode. VDOM2 is operating in NAT mode. There is an inter-VDOM link between both VDOMs. A client workstation with the IP address 10.0.1.10/24 is connected to portA web server with the IP address 10.200.1.2/24 is connected to port1.

Which two options must be included in the FortiGate configuration to route and allow connections from the client workstation to the web server? (Choose two.)

1. A static or dynamic route in VDOM2 with the subnet 10.0.1.0/24 as the destination.
2. A static or dynamic route in VDOM1 with the subnet 10.200.1.0/24 as the destination.
3. One firewall policy in VDOM1 with port2 as the source interface and InterVDOM0 as the destination interface.
4. One firewall policy in VDOM2 with InterVDOM1 as the source interface and port1 as the destination interface.

Correct Answer(s): 3, 4

Question #28

NGFW mode allows policy-based configuration for most inspection rules.

Which security profile configuration does not change when you enable policy-based inspection?

1. Application control
2. Web filtering
3. Web proxy
4. Antivirus

Correct Answer(s): 4

Question #29

Which two statements about the firmware upgrade process on an active-active HA cluster are true? (Choose two.)

1. The firmware image must be uploaded manually to each FortiGate.
2. Uninterruptable upgrade is enabled by default.
3. Traffic load balancing is temporarily disabled while the firmware is upgraded.
4. Only secondary FortiGate devices are rebooted.

Correct Answer(s): 2, 3

Question #30

Which statement about the firewall policy authentication timeout is true?

1. It is an idle timeout. The FortiGate considers a user to be "idle" if it does not see any packets coming from the user's source IP.
2. It is a hard timeout. The FortiGate removes the temporary policy for a user's source IP address after this timer has expired.
3. It is an idle timeout. The FortiGate considers a user to be "idle" if it does not see any packets coming from the user's source MAC.
4. It is a hard timeout. The FortiGate removes the temporary policy for a user's source MAC address after this timer has expired.

Correct Answer(s): 1

Question #31

Which two statements correctly describe how FortiGate performs route lookup, when searching for a suitable gateway? (Choose two.)

1. Lookup is done on the first packet from the session originator
2. Lookup is done on the last packet sent from the responder
3. Lookup is done on every packet, regardless of direction
4. Lookup is done on the first reply packet from the responder

Correct Answer(s): 1, 4

Question #32

A FortiGate is operating in NAT mode and configured with two virtual LAN (VLAN) subinterfaces added to the physical interface.

In this scenario, which statement about the VLAN IDs is true?

1. The two VLAN sub interfaces can have the same VLAN ID, only if they have IP addresses in different subnets.
2. The two VLAN sub interfaces must have different VLAN IDs.
3. The two VLAN sub interfaces can have the same VLAN ID, only if they belong to different VDOMs.
4. The two VLAN sub interfaces can have the same VLAN ID, only if they have IP addresses in the same subnet.

Correct Answer(s): 2

Question #33

Refer to the exhibit.

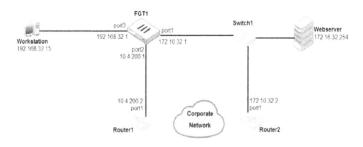

Given the network diagram shown in the exhibit, which route is the best candidate route for FGT1 to route traffic from the workstation to the webserver?

1. 172.16.32.0/24 is directly connected, port1

20

2. 172.16.0.0/16 [50/0] via 10.4.200.2, port2 [5/0]
3. 10.4.200.0/30 is directly connected, port2
4. 0.0.0.0/0 [20/0] via 10.4.200.2, port2

Correct Answer(s): 1

Question #34

Which two statements about central NAT are true? (Choose two.)

1. SNAT using central NAT does not require a central SNAT policy.
2. Central NAT can be enabled or disabled from the CLI only.
3. IP pool references must be removed from existing firewall policies, before enabling central NAT.
4. DNAT using central NAT requires a VIP object as the destination address in a firewall policy.

Correct Answer(s): 2, 3

Question #35

Which condition must be met in order for a web browser to trust a web server certificate signed by a third-party CA?

1. The private key of the CA certificate that is signing the browser certificate must be installed on the browser.
2. The CA certificate that signed the web server certificate must be installed on the browser.
3. The public key of the web server certificate must be installed on the web browser.
4. The web-server certificate must be installed on the browser.

Correct Answer(s): 2

Question #36

Refer to the exhibit.

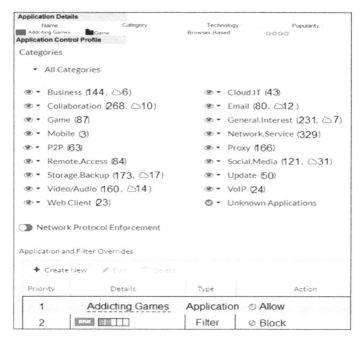

A user located behind the FortiGate device is trying to go to http://www.addictinggames.com (Addicting.Games). The exhibit shows the application details and application control profile.

Based on this configuration, which statement is true?

1. Addicting.Games will be blocked, based on the Filter Overrides configuration.

2. Addicting.Games will be allowed only if the Filter Overrides action is set to Learn.
3. Addicting.Games will be allowed, based on the Categories configuration.
4. Addicting.Games will be allowed, based on the Application Overrides configuration.

Correct Answer(s): 4

Question #37

Refer to the exhibit.

```
config authentication setting
    set active-auth-scheme SCHEME1
end
config authentication rule
    edit WebProxyRule
      set srcaddr 10.0.1.0/24
      set active-auth-method SCHEME2
    next
end
```

The exhibit shows a FortiGate configuration.

How does FortiGate handle web proxy traffic coming from the IP address 10.2.1.200, that requires authorization?

1. It always authorizes the traffic without requiring authentication.
2. It drops the traffic
3. It authenticates the traffic using the authentication scheme SCHEME2.
4. It authenticates the traffic using the authentication scheme SCHEME1.

Correct Answer(s): 4

Question #38

Which statement about the IP authentication header (AH) used by IPsec is true?

1. AH does not support perfect forward secrecy.
2. AH provides strong data integrity but weak encryption.
3. AH provides data integrity but no encryption.
4. AH does not provide any data integrity or encryption.

Correct Answer(s): 3

Question #39

Refer to the exhibits.

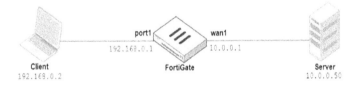

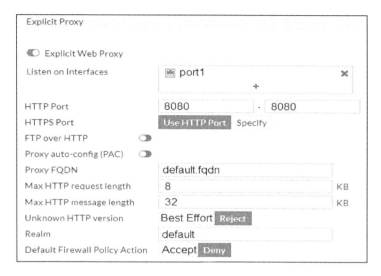

The exhibits show a network diagram and the explicit web proxy configuration.

In the command diagnose sniffer packet, what filter can you use to capture the traffic between the client and the explicit web proxy?

1. "'host 192.168.0.2 and port 8080'
2. 'host 10.0.0.50 and port 80'"
3. "'host 192.168.0.1 and port 80'
4. 'host 10.0.0.50 and port 8080'"

Correct Answer(s): 1

Question #40

How do you format the FortiGate flash disk?

1. Execute the CLI command execute formatlogdisk.
2. Select the format boot device option from the BIOS menu.

3. Load the hardware test (HQIP) image.
4. Load a debug FortiOS image.

Correct Answer(s): 2

Question #41

If the Services field is configured in a Virtual IP (VIP), which statement is true when central NAT is used?

1. The Services field prevents SNAT and DNAT from being combined in the same policy.
2. The Services field is used when you need to bundle several VIPs into VIP groups.
3. The Services field removes the requirement to create multiple VIPs for different services.
4. The Services field prevents multiple sources of traffic from using multiple services to connect to a single computer.

Correct Answer(s): 3

Question #42

Which three types of traffic and attacks can be blocked by a web application firewall (WAF) profile? (Choose three.)

1. Server information disclosure attacks
2. Traffic to botnet servers
3. Credit card data leaks
4. Traffic to inappropriate web sites
5. SQL injection attacks

Correct Answer(s): 1, 3, 5

Question #43

Why does FortiGate keep TCP sessions in the session table for several seconds, even after both sides (client and server) have terminated the session?

1. To generate logs
2. To remove the NAT operation
3. To finish any inspection operations
4. To allow for out-of-order packets that could arrive after the FIN/ACK packets

Correct Answer(s): 4

Question #44

Examine this PAC file configuration.

```
function FindProxyForURL (url, host) {
if (shExpMatch (url, "*.fortinet.com/*")) {
return "DIRECT";}
if (isInNet (host, "172.25.120.0", "255.255.255.0")) {
return "PROXY altproxy.corp.com: 8060";) }
return "PROXY proxy.corp.com:8090";
}
```

Which of the following statements are true? (Choose two.)

1. Browsers can be configured to retrieve this PAC file from FortiGate.
2. Any web request sent to the 172.25.120.0/24 subnet is allowed to bypass the proxy.
3. All requests not sent to fortinet.com or the 172.25.120.0/24 subnet, have to go through altproxy.corp.com: 8060.

4. Any web request sent to fortinet.com is allowed to bypass the proxy.

Correct Answer(s): 1, 4

Question #45

Which two statements correctly describe auto discovery VPN (ADVPN)? (Choose two.)

1. IPSec tunnels are negotiated dynamically between spokes.
2. ADVPN is supported only with IKEv2.
3. It recommends the use of dynamic routing protocols, so that spokes can learn the routes to other spokes.
4. Every spoke requires a static tunnel to be configured to other spokes, so that phase 1 and phase 2 proposals are defined in advance.

Correct Answer(s): 1, 3

Question #46

Refer to the exhibit.

Given to the static routes shown in the exhibit, which statements are correct? (Choose two.)

1. This is a redundant IPsec setup.
2. This setup requires at least two firewall policies with the action set to IPsec.
3. Dead peer detection must be disabled to support this type of IPsec setup.
4. The TunnelB route is the primary route for reaching the remote site. The TunnelA route is used only if the TunnelB VPN is down.

Correct Answer(s): 1, 4

Question #47

To complete the final step of a Security Fabric configuration, an administrator must authorize all the devices on which device?

1. FortiManager
2. Root FortiGate
3. FortiAnalyzer
4. Downstream FortiGate

Correct Answer(s): 32

Question #48

If the Issuer and Subject values are the same in a digital certificate, to which type of entity was the certificate issued?

1. A subordinate CA
2. A root CA

3. A user
4. A CRL

Correct Answer(s): 2

Question #49

Examine the output from a debug flow:

```
id=20085 trace_id=1 func=print_pkt_detail line=5363 msg="vd-root received a packet(proto=1,
10.0.1.10:1->10.200.1.254:2048)
from port3. type=8, code=0, id=1, seq=33."
id=20085 trace_id=1 func=init_ip_session_common line=5519 msg="allocate a new session=00000340"
id=20085 trace_id=1 func=vf_ip_route_input_common line=2583 msg="find a route: flag=04000000 gw-10.200.1.254 via
port1"
id=20085 trace_id=1 func=fw_forward_handler line=586 msg="Denied by forward policy check (policy 0)"
```

Why did the FortiGate drop the packet?

1. The next-hop IP address is unreachable.
2. It failed the RPF check.
3. It matched an explicitly configured firewall policy with the action DENY.
4. It matched the default implicit firewall policy.

Correct Answer(s): 4

Question #50

An administrator has configured the following settings:

```
config system settings
set ses-denied-traffic enable
end
config system global
set block-session-timer 30
end
```

What are the two results of this configuration? (Choose two.)

1. Device detection on all interfaces is enforced for 30 minutes.
2. Denied users are blocked for 30 minutes.
3. A session for denied traffic is created.
4. The number of logs generated by denied traffic is reduced.

Correct Answer(s): 3, 4

Question #51

Refer to the exhibit.

```
date=2017-08-31 time=12:50:06 logid=0316013057 type=utm subtype=webfilter eventtype=ftgd_blk
level=warning vd=root policyid=1 sessionid=149645 user= "" srcip=10.0.1.10 srcport=52919
srcintf="port3" dstip=54.230.128.169 dstport=80 dstinf= "port1" proto=6 service= "HTTP"
hostname= "miniclip.com" profile= "default" action=blocked reqtype=direct url= "/" sentbyte=286
rcvdbyte=0 direction=outgoing msg= "URL belongs to a category with warnings enabled"
method=dcmain cat=20 catdesc= "Games" crscore=30 crlevel=high
```

The exhibit shows a web filtering log.

Which statement about the log message is true?

1. The web site miniclip.com matches a static URL filter whose action is set to Warning.
2. The usage quota for the IP address 10.0.1.10 has expired.
3. The action for the category Games is set to block.
4. The name of the applied web filter profile is default.

Correct Answer(s): 4

Question #52

Which two statements about firewall policy NAT using the outgoing interface IP address with fixed port disabled are true? (Choose two.)

1. The source IP is translated to the outgoing interface IP.
2. This is known as many-to-one NAT.
3. Port address translation is not used.
4. Connections are tracked using source port and source MAC address.

Correct Answer(s): 1, 2

Question #53

Refer to the exhibit.

Field	Value
Version	V3
Serial Number	98765432
Signature algorithm	SHA256RSA
Issuer	cn=RootCA,o=BridgeAuthority, Inc., c=US
Valid from	Tuesday, October 3, 2016 4:33:37 PM
Valid to	Wednesday, October 2, 2019 5:03:37 PM
Subject	cn=John Doe, o=ABC. Inc.,c=US
Public key	RSA (2048 bits)
Key Usage	keyCertSign
Extended Key Usage	Server Authentication (1.3.6.1.5.5.7.3.1), Client Authentication (1.3.6.1.5.5.7.3.2)
Basic Constraints	CA=True, Path Constraint=None
CRL Distribution Points	URL=http://webserver.abcinc.com/arlcert.crl

According to the certificate values shown in the exhibit, which type of entity was the certificate issued to?

1. A user
2. A root CA
3. A bridge CA
4. A subordinate

Correct Answer(s): 1

Question #54

Which two actions are valid for a FortiGuard category-based filter, in a web filter profile, for a firewall policy in proxy-based inspection mode? (Choose two.)

1. Learn
2. Exempt
3. Allow
4. Warning

Correct Answer(s): 3, 4

Question #55

Which two options are purposes of NAT traversal in IPsec? (Choose two.)

1. To force a new DH exchange with each phase 2 rekey
2. To detect intermediary NAT devices in the tunnel path
3. To encapsulate ESP packets in UDP packets using port 4500
4. To dynamically change phase 1 negotiation mode to aggressive mode

Correct Answer(s): 2, 3

Question #56

An administrator has configured a route-based IPsec VPN between two FortiGate devices.

Which statement about this IPsec VPN configuration is true?

1. A phase 2 configuration is not required.
2. This VPN cannot be used as part of a hub-and-spoke topology.
3. A virtual IPsec interface is automatically created after the phase 1 configuration is completed.
4. The IPsec firewall policies must be placed at the top of the list.

Correct Answer(s): 3

Question #57

What is the limitation of using a URL list and application control on the same firewall policy, in NGFW policy-based mode?

1. It limits the scope of application control to scan traffic based on the browser-based technology category only.
2. It limits the scope of application control to scan application traffic based on application category only.
3. It limits the scope of application control to scan application traffic using parent signatures only
4. It limits the scope of application control to scan application traffic on DNS protocol only.

Correct Answer(s): 1

Question #58

An administrator is configuring an IPsec VPN between site A and site B. The Remote Gateway setting in both sites has been configured as Static IP Address.

For site A, the local quick mode selector is 192.168.1.0/24 and the remote quick mode selector is 192.168.2.0/24.

Which subnet must the administrator configure for the local quick mode selector for site B?

1. 192.168.1.0/24
2. 192.168.0.0/8
3. 192.168.2.0/24
4. 192.168.3.0/24

Correct Answer(s): 3

Question #59

Refer to the exhibits.

The exhibits show the IPS sensor and DoS policy configuration.

When detecting attacks, which anomaly, signature, or filter will FortiGate evaluate first?

1. ip_src_session
2. IMAP.Login.Brute.Force
3. Location: server Protocol:SMTP
4. SMTP.Login.Brute.Force

Correct Answer(s): 1

Question #60

Which of the following statements about backing up logs from the CLI and downloading logs from the GUI are true? (Choose two.)

1. Log downloads from the GUI are limited to the current filter view
2. Log backups from the CLI cannot be restored to another FortiGate.
3. Log backups from the CLI can be configured to upload to FTP as a scheduled time
4. Log downloads from the GUI are stored as LZ4 compressed files.

Correct Answer(s): 1, 2

Question #61

Refer to the exhibit.

Status	Name	VLAN ID	Type	IP/Netmask
Physical(12)				
○	port1		Physical Interface	10.200.1.1 255.255.255.0
	port1-VLAN1	1	VLAN	10.200.5.1 255.255.255.0
	port1-VLAN10	10	VLAN	10.0.10.1 255.255.255.0
○	port2		Physical Interface	10.200.2.1 255.255.255.0
	port2-VLAN1	1	VLAN	10.0.5.1 255.255.255.0
	port2-VLAN10	10	VLAN	10.0.20.254 255.255.255.0
○	port3		Physical Interface	10.0.1.254 255.255.255.0

Given the FortiGate interfaces shown in the exhibit, which two statements about the FortiGate interfaces configuration in the exhibit are true? (Choose two.)

1. Traffic between port1-VLAN1 and port2-VLAN1 is allowed by default.
2. Broadcast traffic received on port1-VLAN10 will not be forwarded to port2-VLAN10
3. port1-VLAN10 and port2-VLAN10 can be assigned to different VDOMs.
4. port1-VLAN1 is the native VLAN for the port1 physical interface.

Correct Answer(s): 2, 3

Question #62

When browsing to an internal web server using a web-mode SSL VPN bookmark, which IP address is used as the source of the HTTP request?

1. The remote user's virtual IP address
2. The public IP address of the FortiGate device
3. The remote user's public IP address
4. The internal IP address of the FortiGate device

Correct Answer(s): 4

Question #63

An administrator observes that the port1 inteface cannot be configured with an IP address.

What are three possible reasons for this? (Choose three.)

1. The operation mode is transparent.
2. The interface is a member of a virtual wire pair.
3. The interface is a member of a zone.
4. The interface has been configured for one-arm sniffer.
5. Captive portal is enabled in the interface.

Correct Answer(s): 1, 2, 4

Question #64

Refer to the exhibits.

Firewall Policies

ID	Name	Source	Destination	Schedule	Service	Action	NAT
⊟ 🖼 LAN(port2)→ 🖼 WAN(port1) ❶							
1	Full_Access	🖳 all	🖳 all	🕒 always	🔲 ALL	✔ ACCEPT	✔ Enabled
⊟ 🖼 WAN(port 1)→ 🖼 LAN(port 2) ❶							
2	WebServer	🖳 all	🖳 VIP	🕒 always	🔲 ALL	✔ ACCEPT	⊗ Disabled

The exhibits contain a network diagram and virtual IP and firewall policy configuration.

The WAN (port1) interface has the IP address 10.200.1.1/2The LAN (port2) interface has the IP address 10.0.1.254/24.

The first firewall policy has NAT enabled on the outgoing interface address. The second firewall policy is configured with a VIP as the destination address.

Which IP address will be used to source NAT the Internet traffic coming from a workstation with the IP address 10.0.1.10/32?

1. Any available IP address in the WAN (port1) subnet 10.200.1.0/24
2. 10.200.1.10
3. 10.200.1.1
4. 10.0.1.254

Correct Answer(s): 3

Question #65

Refer to the exhibit.

FortiGate Configuration

```
config system global

    set av-failopen pass

end
```

Debug command output

```
# diagnose hardware sysinfo conserve

memory conserve mode: on

total RAM: 3040 MB

memory used: 2948 MB 97% of total RAM

memory freeable: 92 MB 3% of total RAM

memory used + freeable threshold extreme: 2887 MB 95% of total RAM

memory used threshold red: 2675 MB 88% of total RAM

memory used threshold green: 2492 MB 82% of total RAM
```

The exhibit shows FortiGate configuration and the output of the debug command.

Based on the diagnostic output, how is the FortiGate handling the traffic for new sessions that require proxy based inspection?

1. It is allowed, but with no inspection.
2. It is allowed and inspected, as long as the only inspection required is antivirus.
3. It is dropped.
4. It is allowed and inspected, as long as the inspection is flow based.

Correct Answer(s): 3

Question #66

Which statement about SSL VPN settings for an SSL VPN portal is true?

1. By default, DNS split tunneling is enabled.
2. By default, the admin GUI and the SSL VPN portal use the same HTTPS port.
3. By default, the SSL VPN portal requires the installation of a client's certificate.
4. By default, FortiGate uses WINS servers to resolve names.

Correct Answer(s): 2

Question #67

Refer to the exhibit.

+ Create New ✏ Edit 🔳 Clone 🗑 Delete				
▼ Destination ⌄	▼ Gateway ⌄	▼ Interface ⌄	▼ Priority ⌄	▼ Distance ⌄
172 20 168 0/24	172 25 176 1	⊳ port1	10	20
172 20 168 0/24	172 25 178 1	⊳ port2	20	20

The exhibit shows two static routes.

Which option accurately describes how FortiGate will handle these two routes to the same destination?

1. FortiGate will only activate the port1 route in the routing table.
2. FortiGate will use the port1 route as the primary candidate.
3. FortiGate will load balance all traffic across both routes.
4. FortiGate will route twice as much traffic to the port2 route.

Correct Answer(s): 2

Question #68

Refer to the exhibit.

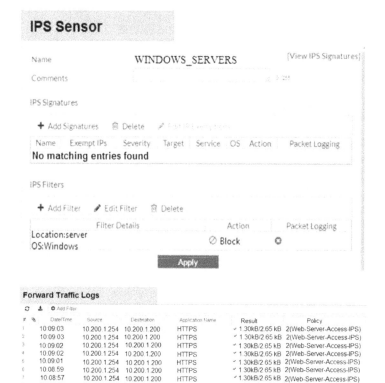

The exhibit shows the IPS sensor configuration and forward traffic logs.

An administrator has configured the WINDOWS_SERVERS IPS sensor in an attempt to determine whether the influx of HTTPS traffic is an attack attempt, or not.

After applying the IPS sensor, FortiGate is still not generating any IPS logs for the HTTPS traffic.

1. What is a possible reason for this?
2. The HTTPS signatures have not been added to the sensor.
3. The IPS filter is missing the Protocol:HTTPS option.
4. The firewall policy is not using a full SSL inspection profile.
5. A DoS policy should be used, instead of an IPS sensor.

Correct Answer(s): 3

Question #69

Which two SD-WAN load balancing methods use interface weight value to distribute traffic?

1. Spillover
2. Volume
3. Source IP
4. Sessions

Correct Answer(s): 2, 4

Question #70

Which certificate value can FortiGate use to determine the relationship between the issuer and the certificate?

1. Subject Key Identifier value
2. SMMIE Capabilities value
3. Subject value
4. Subject Alternative Name value

Correct Answer(s): 3

Question #71

Why must you use aggressive mode when a local FortiGate IPsec gateway hosts multiple dialup tunnels?

1. Main mode does not support XAuth for user authentication.
2. In aggressive mode, the remote peers are able to provide their peer IDs in the first message.
3. FortiGate is able to handle NATed connections only in aggressive mode.
4. FortiClient supports only aggressive mode.

Correct Answer(s): 2

Question #72

Which statement about the policy ID number of a firewall policy is true?

1. It is required to modify a firewall policy using the CLI.
2. It represents the number of objects used in the firewall policy.
3. It changes when firewall policies are reordered.
4. It defines the order in which rules are processed.

Correct Answer(s): 1

Question #73

Which two settings must you configure to ensure FortiGate generates logs for web filter activity on a firewall policy called Full Access? (Choose two.)

1. Enable Event Logging.
2. Enable disk logging.
3. Enable a web filter security profile on the Full Access firewall policy.
4. Enable Log Allowed Traffic on the Full Access firewall policy.

Correct Answer(s): 3, 4

Question #74

An administrator is running the following sniffer command:

diagnose sniffer packet any "host 10.0.2.10" 3

Which three items will be included in the sniffer output? (Choose three.)

1. IP header
2. Interface name
3. Packet payload
4. Ethernet header
5. Application header

Correct Answer(s): 1, 3, 4

Question #75

Refer to the exhibit.

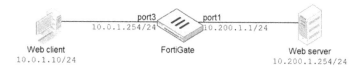

In the network shown in the exhibit, the web client cannot connect to the HTTP web server. The administrator runs the FortiGate built-in sniffer and gets the following output:

FortiGate # diagnose sniffer packet any "port 80" 4

interfaces=[any]

filters=[port 80]

11.510058 port3 in 10.0.1.10.49255 ->

10.200.1.254.80: syn 697263124

11.760531 port3 in 10.0.1.10.49256 ->

10.200.1.254.80: syn 868017830

14.505371 port3 in 10.0.1.10.49255 ->

10.200.1.254.80: syn 697263124

14.755510 port3 in 10.0.1.10.49256 ->

10.200.1.254.80: syn 868017830

What should the administrator do next to troubleshoot the problem?

1. Capture the traffic using an external sniffer connected to port1.
2. Run a sniffer on the web server.
3. Execute another sniffer in the FortiGate, this time with the filter, "host 10.0.1.10".
4. Execute a debug flow.

47

Correct Answer(s): 4

Question #76

Refer to the exhibit:

```
FGT1 # get router info routing-table database
Codes: K - kernel, C - connected, S - static, R - RIP, B - BGP
       O - OSPF, IA - OSPF inter area
       N1 - OSPF NSSA external type 1, N2 - OSPF NSSA external type 2
       E1 - OSPF external type 1, E2 - OSPF external type 2
       i - IS-IS, L1 - IS-IS level-1, L2 - IS-IS level-2, ia - IS-IS inter area
       > - selected route, * - FIB route, p - stale info

S    *> 0.0.0.0/0 [10/0] via 172.20.121.2, port1, [20/0]
     *>           [10/0] via 10.0.0.2, port2, [30/0]
S       0.0.0.0/0 [20/0] via 192.168.15.2, port3, [10/0]
C    *> 10.0.0.0/24 is directly connected, port2
S       172.13.24.0/24 [10/0] is directly connected, port4
C    *> 172.20.121.0/24 is directly connected, port1
S    *> 192.167.1.0/24 [10/0] via 10.0.0.2, port2
C    *> 192.168.15.0/24 is directly connected, port3
```

Given the routing database shown in the exhibit, which two statements are correct? (Choose two.)

1. The port3 default route has the lowest metric.
2. The port3 default route has the highest distance.
3. There will be eight routes active in the routing table.
4. The port1 and port2 default routes are active in the routing table.

Correct Answer(s): 2, 4

Question #77

Refer to the exhibit.

Admission Control

Security Mode	Captive Portal ▾
Authentication Portal	**Local** External
User Access ℹ	Restricted to Groups **Allow all**

The exhibit shows admission control settings.

Which users and user groups are allowed access to the network through captive portal?

1. Groups defined in the captive portal configuration
2. Only individual users "" not groups "" defined in the captive portal configuration
3. All users
4. Users and groups defined in the firewall policy

Correct Answer(s): 4

Question #78

Which two configuration objects can you select in for the Source field of a firewall policy? (Choose two.)

1. Firewall service
2. FQDN address
3. IP pool
4. User or user group

Correct Answer(s): 2, 4

Question #79

Which actions can be applied to each filter in the application control profile?

1. Block, monitor, warning, and quarantine
2. Allow, monitor, block, and learn
3. Allow, monitor, block, and quarantine
4. Allow, block, authenticate, and warning

Correct Answer(s): 3

Question #80

How does FortiGate select the central SNAT policy that is applied to a TCP session?

1. It selects the first matching central SNAT policy, reviewing from top to bottom.
2. It selects the SNAT policy specified in the configuration of the outgoing interface.
3. It selects the SNAT policy specified in the configuration of the firewall policy that matches the traffic.
4. It selects the central SNAT policy with the lowest priority

Correct Answer(s): 1

Question #81

Refer to the exhibit.

```
Local-FortiGate # diagnose sys ha checksum cluster

================= FGVM010000058290 =================

is_manage_master()=1, is_root_master()=1
debugzone
global: 85 26 52 f2 f9 6e 3c c9 f5 21 1a 78 69 b6 20 bd
root: 30 51 63 1b 2d ef 77 aa f7 50 00 25 4d 42 a9 7d
all: 38 28 3d e4 24 8f 5b 10 8a 64 30 f2 34 13 c1 35

checksum
global: 85 26 52 f2 f9 6e 3c c9 f5 21 1a 78 69 b6 20 bd
root: 30 51 63 1b 2d ef 77 aa f7 50 00 25 4d 42 a9 7d
all: 38 28 3d e4 24 8f 5b 10 8a 64 30 f2 34 13 c1 35

================= FGVM010000058289 =================

is_manage_master()=0, is_root_master()=0
debugzone
global: 85 26 52 f2 f9 6e 3c c9 f5 21 1a 78 69 b6 20 bd
root: 30 51 63 1b 2d ef 77 aa f7 50 00 25 4d 8a 55 8b
all: 38 28 3d e4 24 8f 5b 10 8a 64 30 f2 34 dc 9a 43

checksum
global: 85 26 52 f2 f9 6e 3c c9 f5 21 1a 78 69 b6 20 bd
root: 30 51 63 1b 2d ef 77 aa f7 50 00 25 4d 8a 55 8b
all: 38 28 3d e4 24 8f 5b 10 8a 64 30 f2 34 dc 9a 43
```

Given the output of the # diagnose sys ha checksum cluster command shown in the exhibit, which two statements are correct? (Choose two.)

1. The all VDOM is not synchronized between the primary and secondary FortiGate devices.
2. The global configuration is synchronized between the primary and secondary FortiGate devices.
3. The root VDOM is not synchronized between the primary and secondary FortiGate devices.
4. The FortiGate devices have three VDOMs.

Correct Answer(s): 2, 3

Question #82

Which two statements about DNS filter profiles are true? (Choose two.)

1. They can block DNS requests to known botnet command and control servers
2. They can inspect HTTP traffic.
3. They must be applied in firewall policies with SSL inspection enabled
4. They can redirect blocked requests to a specific portal

Correct Answer(s): 2, 4

Question #83

An administrator needs to strengthen the security for SSL VPN access.

Which three statements are best practices to do so? (Choose three.)

1. Configure a client integrity check (host-check)
2. Configure two-factor authentication using security certificates.
3. Configure split tunneling
4. Configure host restrictions by IP address or by MAC address.
5. Configure SSL offloading to a content processor.

Correct Answer(s): 1, 2, 4

Question #84

Refer to the exhibit.

```
# diagnose sys session stat
misc info: session_count=16 setup_rate=0 exp_count=0 clash=889
memory_tension_drop=0 ephemeral=1/16384 removeable=3
delete=0, flush=0, dev_down=16/69
firewall error stat:
error1=00000000
error2=00000000
error3=00000000
error4=00000000
tt=00000000
cont=0005e722
ids_recv=000fdc94
url_recv=00000000
av_recv=001fee47
fqdn_count=00000000
tcp reset stat: syncqf=119 acceptqf=0 no-listener=3995 data=0 ses=2 ips=0
global: ses_limit=0 ses6_limit=0 rt_limit=0 rt6_limit=0
```

An administrator is investigating a report of users having intermittent issues with browsing the web. The administrator ran diagnostics and received the output shown in the exhibit.

Which option is the most likely cause of the issue?

1. High session timeout value
2. High memory usage
3. High CPU usage
4. NAT port exhaustion

Correct Answer(s): 4

Question #85

Which process is involved in updating IPS from FortiGuard?

1. IPS engine updates can be obtained using only push updates.
2. FortiGate IPS update requests are sent using UDP port 443.
3. IPS signature update requests are sent to update.fortiguard.net.
4. Protocol decoder update requests are sent to sevice.fortiguard.net.

Correct Answer(s): 3

Question #86

Which two conditions are required for establishing an IPsec VPN between two FortiGate devices? (Choose two.)

1. If the VPN is configured as policy-based in one peer, it must also be configured as policy-based in the other peer.
2. If the VPN is configured as DialUp User in one peer, it must be configured as either Static IP Address or Dynamic DNS in the other peer.
3. If XAuth is enabled as a server in one peer, it must be enabled as a client in the other peer.
4. If the VPN is configured as route-based, there must be at least one firewall policy with the action set to IPsec.

Correct Answer(s): 2, 3

Question #87

Refer to the exhibit.

```
config system interface
  edit "VLAN10"
        set vdom "VDOM1"
        set forward-domain 100
        set role lan
        set interface "port9"
        set vlanid 10
    next
    edit "VLAN5"
        set vdom "VDOM1"
        set forward-domain 50
        set role lan
        set interface "port10"
        set vlanid 5
    next
  end
```

The exhibit shows the two VLAN interfaces configuration.

A DHCP server is connected to the VLAN10 interface. A DHCP client is connected to the VLAN5 interface. However, the DHCP client cannot get a dynamic IP address from the DHCP server.

What condition must exist in order for the DHCP client to successfully get the dynamic IP address?

1. Both interfaces must belong to the same forward domain.
2. Both interfaces must have the same VLAN ID.
3. The role of the VLAN10 interface must be set to server.
4. Both interfaces must be in different VDOMs.

Correct Answer(s): 1

Question #88

Refer to the exhibit.

The exhibit contains a proxy address that an administrator created to block HTTP uploads.

Where must the proxy address be used?

1. As the source in a firewall policy
2. As the destination in a firewall policy
3. As the destination in a proxy policy
4. As the source in a proxy policy

Correct Answer(s): 4

Question #89

An administrator has configured central DNAT and virtual IPs.

Which object can be selected in the firewall policy Destination field?

1. The mapped IP address object of the VIP object
2. A VIP group object
3. A VIP object
4. An IP pool object

Correct Answer(s): 1

Question #90

By default, when logging to disk, when does FortiGate delete logs?

1. Never
2. 7 days
3. 1 year
4. 30 days

Correct Answer(s): 2

Question #91

Which two statements about HA for FortiGate devices are true? (Choose two.)

1. Virtual clustering can be configured between two FortiGate devices that have multiple VDOMs.
2. HA management interface settings are synchronized between cluster members.

3. Heartbeat interfaces are not required on the primary device.
4. Sessions handled by proxy-based security profiles cannot be synchronized.

Correct Answer(s): 1, 4

Question #92

How can you block or allow access to Twitter using a firewall policy?

1. Configure the Service field as Internet Service objects for Twitter.
2. Configure the Source field as Internet Service objects for Twitter
3. Configure the Action field as Learn and select Twitter.
4. Configure the Destination field as Internet Service objects for Twitter.

Correct Answer(s): 43

Question #93

Which statement about FortiGuard services for FortiGate is true?

1. The web filtering database is downloaded locally on FortiGate.
2. FortiGate downloads IPS updates using UDP port 53 or 8888.
3. Antivirus signatures are downloaded locally on FortiGate.
4. FortiAnalyzer can be configured as a local FDN to provide antivirus and IPS updates.

Correct Answer(s): 3

Question #94

How does FortiGate verify the login credentials of a remote LDAP user?

1. FortiGate queries its own database for credentials.
2. FortiGate queries the LDAP server for credentials.
3. FortiGate sends the user-entered credentials to the LDAP server for authentication.
4. FortiGate regenerates the algorithm based on the login credentials and compares it to the algorithm stored on the LDAP server.

Correct Answer(s): 3

Question #95

When using SD-WAN, how must you configure a next-hop gateway address for a member interface, so that FortiGate can forward Internet traffic?

1. It must be configured in a policy route using the sdwan virtual interface.
2. It must be learned automatically through a dynamic routing protocol.
3. It must be configured in a static route using the sdwan virtual interface.
4. It must be provided in the SD-WAN member interface configuration.

Correct Answer(s): 4

Question #96

Which statement about the FSSO collector agent timers is true?

1. The workstation verify interval is used to periodically check if a workstation is still a domain member.
2. The dead entry timeout interval is used to age out entries with an unverified status.
3. The user group cache expiry is used to age out the monitored groups.
4. The IP address change verify interval monitors the server IP address where the collector agent is installed.

Correct Answer(s): 2

Question #97

Which two statements describe WMI polling mode for the FSSO collector agent? (Choose two.)

1. WMI polling can increase bandwidth usage in large networks.
2. The NetSessionEnum function is used to track user logoffs.
3. The collector agent does not need to search any security event logs.
4. The collector agent uses a Windows API to query DCs for user logins.

Correct Answer(s): 3, 4

Question #98

Refer to the exhibit.

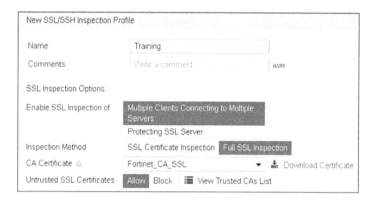

An employee connects to https://example.com using a web browser. The web server's certificate was signed by a private internal CA. The FortiGate that is inspecting this traffic is configured for full SSL inspection.

The exhibit shows the configuration settings for the SSL/SSH inspection profile that is applied to the policy that is invoked in this instance. All other settings are set to defaults. No certificates have been imported into FortiGate.

Which certificate is presented to the employee's web browser?

1. The web server's certificate
2. The user's personal certificate signed by a private internal CA
3. A certificate signed by Fortinet_CA_SSL
4. A certificate signed by Fortinet_CA_Untrusted

Correct Answer(s): 4

Question #99

An administrator is attempting to allow access to https://fortinet.com through a firewall policy that is configured with a web filter and an SSL inspection profile configured for deep inspection.

Which two actions can eliminate the certificate error generated by deep inspection? (Choose two.)

1. Implement firewall authentication for all users that need access to fortinet.com.
2. Manually install the FortiGate deep inspection certificate as a trusted CA.
3. Configure fortinet.com access to bypass the IPS engine.
4. Configure an SSL-inspection exemption for fortinet.com.

Correct Answer(s): 2, 4

Question #100

Which statement about a One-to-One IP pool is true?

1. It is used for destination NAT.
2. It limits the client to 64 connections per IP pool.
3. It allows the fixed mapping of an internal address range to an external address range.
4. It does not use port address translation.

Correct Answer(s): 4

Question #101

Refer to the exhibit.

The exhibit shows the IPS sensor configuration.

If traffic matches this IPS sensor, which two actions is the sensor expected to take? (Choose two.)

1. The sensor will allow attackers matching the NTP.Spoofed.KoD.DoS signature.
2. The sensor will block all attacks aimed at Windows servers.
3. The sensor will reset all connections that match these signatures.
4. The sensor will gather a packet log for all matched traffic.

Correct Answer(s): 1, 2

Question #102

An administrator wants to throttle the total volume of SMTP sessions to their email server.

Which DoS sensor can the administrator use to achieve this?

1. ip_src_session
2. ip_dst_session

3. udp_flood
4. tcp_port_scan

Correct Answer(s): 2

Question #103

A FortiGate device has multiple VDOMs.

Which statement about an administrator account configured with the default prof_admin profile is true?

1. It can upgrade the firmware on the FortiGate device.
2. It can reset the password for the admin account.
3. It can create administrator accounts with access to the same VDOM.
4. It cannot have access to more than one VDOM.

Correct Answer(s): 3

Question #104

During the digital verification process, comparing the original and fresh hash results satisfies which security requirement?

1. Signature verification
2. Authentication
3. Data integrity
4. Non-deniability

Question #105

Which three statements correctly describe transparent mode operation? (Choose three.)

1. The transparent FortiGate is visible to network hosts in an IP traceroute.
2. FortiGate acts as a transparent bridge and forwards traffic at Layer 2.
3. Ethernet packets are forwarded based on destination MAC addresses, not IP addresses.
4. It permits inline traffic inspection and firewalling without changing the IP scheme of the network.
5. All interfaces on the transparent mode FortiGate device must be on different IP subnets.

Question #106

Which two statements about conserve mode are true? (Choose two.)

1. Administrators can access the FortiGate only through the console port.
2. FortiGate stops doing RPF checks over incoming packets.
3. FortiGate stops sending files to FortiSandbox for inspection.
4. Administrators cannot change the configuration.

Correct Answer(s): 3, 4

Question #107

Which two features are supported by web filter in flow-based inspection mode with NGFW mode set to profile-based? (Choose two.)

1. Search engines
2. FortiGuard Quotas
3. Static URL
4. Rating option

Correct Answer(s): 3, 4

Question #108

Refer to the exhibit.

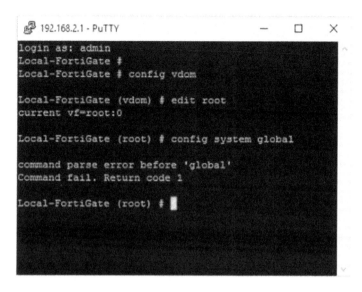

Given the FortiGate CLI output, why is the administrator getting the error shown in the exhibit?

1. The administrator must first enter the command edit global.
2. The administrator admin does not have the privileges required to configure global settings.
3. The command config system global does not exist in FortiGate.
4. The global settings cannot be configured from the root VDOM context.

Correct Answer(s): 4

Question #109

An administrator has configured a dialup IPsec VPN with XAuth.

Which statement best describes what occurs during this scenario?

1. Dialup clients must provide their local ID during phase 2 negotiations.
2. Only digital certificates will be accepted as an authentication method in phase 1.
3. Phase 1 negotiations will skip preshared key exchange.
4. Dialup clients must provide a username and password for authentication.

Correct Answer(s): 4

Question #110

When override is enabled, which option shows the process and selection criteria that is used to elect the primary FortiGate in an HA cluster?

1. Connected monitored ports > HA uptime > priority > serial number
2. HA uptime > priority > Connected monitored ports > serial number
3. Priority > Connected monitored ports > HA uptime > serial number
4. Connected monitored ports > priority > HA uptime > serial number

Correct Answer(s): 4

Question #111

HTTP public key pinning (HPKP) can be an obstacle to implementing full SSL inspection.

In which two ways can you resolve this problem? (Choose two.)

1. Enable Allow Invalid SSL Certificates for the relevant security profile.
2. Exempt those web sites that use HPKP from full SSL inspection.
3. Install the CA certificate (that is required to verify the web server certificate) in the certificate stores of users' computers.
4. Use a web browser that does not support HPKP.

Correct Answer(s): 2, 4

Question #112

A company needs to provide SSL VPN access to two user groups. The company also needs to display a different welcome message for each group, on the SSL

VPN login.

To meet these requirements, what is required in the SSL VPN configuration?

1. Different virtual SSL VPN IP addresses for each group
2. Two separate SSL VPNs in different interfaces mapping the same ssl.root
3. Two firewall policies with different captive portals
4. Different SSL VPN realms for each group

Correct Answer(s): 4

Question #113

Which two route attributes must be equal for static routes to be eligible for equal cost multipath (ECMP) routing? (Choose two.)

1. Metric
2. Priority
3. Cost
4. Distance

Correct Answer(s): 2, 4

Question #114

Which two statements are true when using WPAD with the DHCP discovery method? (Choose two.)

1. If the DHCP method fails, browsers will try the DNS method.
2. The browser sends a DHCPINFORM request to the DHCP server.
3. The DHCP server provides the PAC file for download.
4. The browser needs to be preconfigured with the DHCP server IP address.

Correct Answer(s): 1, 2

Question #115

Refer to the exhibit.

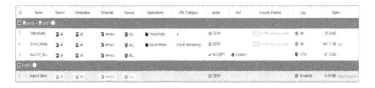

Based on the firewall configuration shown in the exhibit, which two statements about application control behavior are true? (Choose two.)

1. Access to browser-based Social.Media applications will be blocked.
2. Access to mobile social media applications will be blocked.
3. Access to all applications in the Social.Media category will be blocked.
4. Access to all unknown applications will be allowed.

Correct Answer(s): 1, 4

Question #116

Which two statements about SSL VPN timers are true? (Choose two.)

1. SSL VPN settings do not have customizable timers.
2. SSL VPN timers prevent SSL VPN users from being logged out because of high network latency.
3. SSL VPN timers disconnect idle SSL VPN users when a firewall policy authentication timeout occurs.
4. SSL VPN timers allow to mitigate DoS attacks from partial HTTP requests.

Correct Answer(s): 2, 4

Question #117

Refer to the exhibit.

71

```
session info: proto=6 proto_state=01 duration=26 expire=3594 timeout=3600 flags=00000000 sockflag=00000000 sockport=0 av_idx=0 use=4
origin-shaper=
reply-shaper=
per_ip_shaper=
ha_id=0 policy_dir=0 tunnel=/ vlan_cos=0/255
state=may_dirty
statistic(bytes/packets/allow_err): org=1490/14/1 reply=10479/13/1 tuples=2
tx speed(Bps/kbps): 56/0 rx speed(Bps/kbps): 397/3
origin->sink: org pre->post, reply pre->post dev=5->3/3->5 gwy=10.200.1.254/10.0.1.10
hook=post dir=org act=snat 10.0.1.10:60267->52.84.125.124:443(10.200.1.100:60267)
hook=pre dir=reply act=dnat 52.84.125.124:443->10.200.1.100:60267(10.0.1.10:60267)
pos/(before,after) 0/(0,0), 0/(0,0)
misc=0 policy_id=1 auth_info=0 chk_client_info=0 vd=0
serial=00009bd5 tos=ff/ff app_list=0 app=0 url_cat=0
dd_type=0 dd_mode=0
total session 129
```

The exhibit contains a session diagnostic output.

Which statement about the session diagnostic output is true?

1. The session is in CLOSE_WAIT state.
2. The session is in TIME_WAIT state.
3. The session is in LISTEN state.
4. The session is in ESTABLISHED state.

Correct Answer: 4

Question #118

Refer to the exhibit.

```
date=2018-01-30 time=07:21:49 logid="0316013057" type="utm" subtype="webfilter"
eventtype="ftgd_blk" level="warning" vd="root" logtime=1517325709 policyid=1
sessionid=15332 srcip=10.0.1.20 srcport=59538 srcintf="port3" srcintfrole="undefined"
dstip=208.91.112.55 dstport=80 dstintf="port1" dstintfrole="undefined" proto=6
service="HTTP" hostname="lavito.tk" profile="Category-block-and-warning" action="blocked"
reqtype="direct" url="/" sentbyte=140 rcvdbyte=0 direction="outgoing" msg="URL belongs to
a category with warnings enabled" method="domain" cat=0 catdesc="Unrated" crscore=30
crlevel="high"
```

ID	Name	From	To
2	IPS	port1	port3
1	Full_Access	port3	port1
0	Implicit Deny	any	any

The exhibit shows a raw log and firewall policies.

What information does this raw log provide? (Choose two.)

1. type indicates that a security event was recorded.
2. FortiGate blocked the traffic.
3. 10.0.1.20 is the IP address for lavito.tk.
4. policyid indicates that traffic went through the IPS firewall policy.

Correct Answer: 1, 2

Question #119

Which two statements about virtual domains (VDOMs) are true? (Choose two.)

1. A FortiGate device has 64 VDOMs, created by default.
2. The root VDOM is the management VDOM, by default.
3. Each VDOM maintains its own system time.
4. Each VDOM maintains its own routing table.

Correct Answer: 2, 4

www.ingramcontent.com/pod-product-compliance
Lightning Source LLC
Chambersburg PA
CBHW070854070326
40690CB00009B/1835